GRAVEYARD JOKES

That Everyone and Their Dead Ancestors Find Funny!

By Robert Kent
Illustrated by Wesla Weller

Lowell House Juvenile
Los Angeles

Contemporary Books
Chicago

Library of Congress Catalog Card Number: 93-24478

ISBN: 1-56565-101-4

10 9 8 7 6 5 4 3 2

Ready to Dig Up a Body of Jokes?
Enter the Graveyard!

Why did the morticians build a double casket for the zombie funeral?

The body had a date.

Why did the mummy see a psychiatrist?

> *He was coming unwrapped.*

How did Dracula go broke?

> *He emptied out his account at the blood bank.*

Why did Frankenstein visit his mechanic?

> *He needed his bolts tightened.*

What did the mummy's wife wear to the party?

> *Just a little wrap.*

What's a zombie's favorite sitcom?

> *"The Weather Channel."*

What's a ghoul's favorite dessert?

> *Lady fingers.*

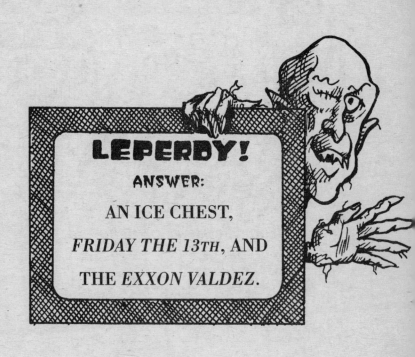

LEPERDY!

ANSWER:

AN ICE CHEST,
FRIDAY THE 13TH, AND
THE *EXXON VALDEZ*.

QUESTION:

WHAT'S A CHILLER,
A THRILLER, AND
A SPILLER?

Why did the old ghouls show up at the cemetery before sundown?

> They didn't want to miss the early bird specials.

What was Lizzie Borden's favorite novel?

I Dismember Mama.

Two flies show up just after a kid threw up.

1st fly: Umm . . . looks like beans and franks for lunch today!

2nd fly: Yum! Do you think we could freeze some of this?

1st fly: Nah. I don't think it would keep.

Where's a creep's favorite vacation spot?

Lake Eerie.

1st ghoul: I'm hungry. Will you go down to the graveyard and get something?

2nd ghoul: Sure. Shall we order some ribs?

1st ghoul: Nah. They're always cold by the time you get them home.

What's the motto of the cannibal fast-food restaurant?

"Over 10 billion customers served."

How did the man going to the electric chair pay for his last meal?

He charged it.

Who is Freddy Krueger's favorite rock star?

Slash.

What's the favorite sitcom down in the tombs?

"Mummy Knows Best."

Gravekeeper: You're sure you want to buy these bodies?

Ghoul: Yes. I'll take six, please.

Gravekeeper: You want me to wrap them up?

Ghoul: No, I'll eat them here.

Why do cannibals love Sundays?

   Because missionaries come
   for dinner.

Quasimodo went to apply for the job of bell ringer at the cathedral. Since there was one other applicant, a competition was set up. Quasimodo went first, taking his mallet and giving the bell a mighty ring. Pleased, he stepped back to let his competitor go next. The fellow rushed the bell, striking it with his head and causing a huge ring. Determined, Quasimodo gave the bell an even greater blow with his mallet, and once again stepped back with satisfaction. Undaunted, his competitor flew madly at the bell. But at the last moment the competitor slipped, missed the bell, and fell off the bell tower to the street below.

When Quasimodo ran down to the street, a policeman asked, "Do you know this man?" Quasimodo replied, "Not really, but his face rings a bell."

What's a mummy's favorite movie?

Mummy Dearest.

Why don't ghouls like to eat internal organs?

They're usually hard to stomach.

How did the mourners look after the cremation?

Ashen.

How do cremators make their money?

They urn it.

What's a zombie's favorite soap opera?

"The Young and the Deathless."

What do you call a vampire teen's allowance for lunch?

Blood money.

What do you get when you cross a werewolf
with a nun?

A nasty habit.

13

Why were the explorers killed when they reached the inside of the pyramid?

> *Because it's not nice to fool with Mummy Nature.*

Bob Ghoul: So, how did the body look at the funeral?

Bill Ghoul: Good enough to eat. Do you want to go to the crematorium for lunch?

Bob Ghoul: No way. They overcook everything.

What do you get when you cross a vampire with a radio announcer?

> *A sucker DJ.*

Why did King Kong climb up the Empire State Building?

> *Because he couldn't take the elevator without a shirt and shoes.*

What do you call an electrocuted crystal ball reader?

Medium-rare.

What's a vampire's least favorite breakfast?

Stake and eggs.

Why did Dracula go to the doctor?

He was coffin too much.

What do you call cattle farms that hire werewolves?

Hairy dairies.

What do you call vomited roast beef?

Up-chuck.

Why did the Bride of Frankenstein's hair turn white?

> *The castle was cold, the food was bad, and she realized she just had married a guy with bolts in his neck.*

Why do zombies often drown at parties?

They always get the instructions for bobbing for apples mixed up.

Why did the mummy go bankrupt?

She got involved in too many pyramid scams.

Why did the mother of the body snatchers yell at them after they dug up two bodies and dragged them to the dinner table?

They were eating with their fingers.

Why did the ghoul family always share the bodies they found?

Because the family that eats together, stays together.

Two flies surround a kid who just got punched in the belly.

1st fly: Looks like this kid got creamed.

2nd fly: Nah, a bully just skimmed a little fat off.

22

Knock knock!

Who's there?

Getyur.

Getyur who?

Getyur fangs outta my neck.

What do ghouls call a burial at noon?

> *Lunch.*

What do ghouls call a burial on a ship?

> *Seafood.*

Knock knock!

Who's there?

Blochunks.

Blochunks who?

**Blochunks in my ear, and I'll follow
you anywhere.**

Why don't nuclear mutants like beach parties?

They hate getting sand in their cores.

What was the theme song from *The Birds?*

> *"Brother, Can You Sparrow a Dime?"*

Why did it take so long to write *The Birds?*

> *The writer didn't know how to type, but he could hunt and peck.*

What do you call a movie about a house haunted by dead rodents?

> *Polter-mice.*

What do you get when you slime a telephone company employee?

> *A smooth operator.*

What's a body snatcher's favorite romantic song?

> *"Why Do Ghouls Fall in Love?"*

Why did so many characters die in *Aliens*?

> *They just couldn't stomach it.*

What do you get when you cross an angry werewolf with a head cold?

> *A booger with an attitude.*

Why don't Venus's-flytraps like beach parties?

They hate getting sand in their buds.

Why don't stabbing victims like beach parties?

They hate getting sand in their slits.

What do you call people who are afraid to go to costume parties?

Hallo-wimpies.

What kind of place does Freddy Krueger have?

A furnaced apartment.

What's Dracula's favorite drink?

A Bloody Mary.

What do you call an indoor home for bats?

Caved Inn.

What do you get when you cross a guillotine with a jockey who has a cold?

A headless hoarse man.

What's the sound a coven of witches makes when they go out at night?

Brr-room, brr-room.

Why was the hideous, man-eating blob turned away at the restaurant?

No shirt, no shoes—no service.

What's a yogi's favorite folk song?

"Way Down upon the Swami River."

What do you get when you cross a drowning victim with a bathroom floor worker?

Tippy canoe and a tiler, too.

What's the difference between a booger and a rich man?

One's a green nosey, and the other knows green.

Why does Frankenstein put on headphones in the morning?

He needs a jump start.

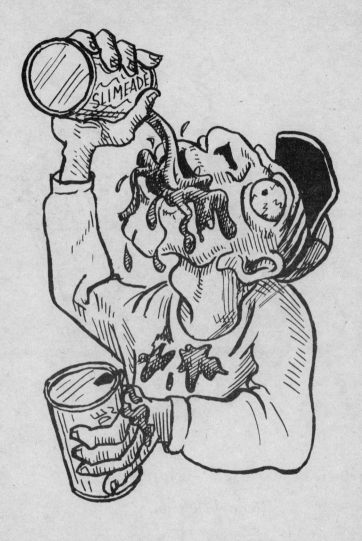

What's the Blob's favorite cold drink?

Slime-ade.

Who is Frankenstein's favorite singer?

Michael Bolt-on.

What do you call Frankenstein when he skips class?

A bolt cutter.

Why was Jack the Ripper thrown out of school?

> *He was such a cut-up.*

What do you call a witty ogre?

> *A droll troll.*

What's the difference between a werewolf and a nasty rabbit?

> *One is a hairy beast, and the other is a beastly hare.*

What do you get when you mix slime with a stack of CDs?

Slipped discs.

What do you call a spirit who gets sliced in half?

A tapered vapor.

Two ghosts were having lunch. The first ghost commented, "Hey, ghosts aren't what they used to be. I saw a ghost help a little old lady cross the road the other day." The second ghost replied, "Was she old and feeble?" The first ghost responded, "Well, not for a ghost!"

What's a cannibal's favorite movie?

Guess Who's Coming for Dinner.

What's a cannibal's second favorite movie?

Breakfast of Tiffany.

Why do cannibals love dinner parties?

> *It gives them a chance to serve loved ones.*

Why did the morticians close the casket at the ghoul's funeral?

> *They didn't want the mourners to stay for dinner.*

Why do zombies love statues?

They can beat them in footraces.

Knock knock!

Who's there?

Ivanna.

Ivanna who?

Ivanna drink your blood.

What do you get when you cross a guillotine with a man riddled with bullet wounds?

> *A headless porous man.*

What's a zombie's favorite song?

> *"Wake Me Up Before You Go-Go."*

Why do cannibals leave lots of room around the body in a funeral home?

> *They need somewhere to put the salad bar.*

Why do zombies get in free at football games?

> *Because they make good yard markers.*

Why do zombies hate ironing their clothes?

> *They can never remember which end of the iron to hold.*

What love song always makes a cyclops cry?

"Smoke Gets in Your Eye."

Why were the guests at the zombie funeral crying?

The body had to leave early.

What's Jack the Ripper's favorite soft drink?

Slice.

What do you get when you cross the San Andreas Fault, Jack the Ripper, and Lizzie Borden?

A crack, a quack, and forty whacks.

Why did Dorothy dream about the Wicked Witch of the West riding a bicycle?

Her broom was in the shop.

Why did Dr. Frankenstein always get Igor to cut the organs out of the bodies?

Because he could really de-liver.

Why do zombies love Mount Rushmore?

> *They're moved by all the emotion.*

Why does the Loch Ness Monster always make hot chocolate for her friends?

> *Because Nessy makes the very best chocolate.*

Why do cannibals love potluck dinners?

> *Because they never know who'll show up for dinner.*

How can you pick out the father at a zombie funeral?

> *He's the one who gives the body away.*

What's a zombie's favorite adventure show?

> *"The Home Shopping Network."*

What do you call a zombie coffin built for four?

A double date.

Why did Godzilla refuse to leave Tokyo, even after destroying it?

Because he wanted to be around for the sequel.

Why do cannibals love dinner by candlelight?

> *Because they're able to see who's being served.*

Why does the Phantom of the Opera haunt an opera house?

> *He was too young to die and too old to rock and roll.*

How can you tell the difference between a zombie funeral and a zombie picnic?

At the picnic you eat, then bury the remains.

Why do cannibals cry at morning funerals?

Because the bodies usually don't last long enough for lunch.

Harriet and Stanley are at their relative's cremation.

Stanley: Uncle George looks so small and pitiful!

Harriet: Dummy! That's Aunt Helen's cigarette ash!

Stanley: Well, it's not going to be the same at the house without Uncle George.

Harriet: What's the difference? He used to be parked in front of the TV, now he's going to be in a vase on top of it.

Why don't vampires like card games?

The stakes usually get too high.

Why do lepers hate bowling?

    They always leave their fingers in the balls.

Why did the cannibals rush home with the pizza delivery boy?

They didn't want dinner to get cold.

Why do witches like to travel on brooms?

Brooms have good mileage, low emissions, and are faster than vacuum cleaners.

What do you get when you cross a banshee with a zombie?

Someone who screams a lot but isn't sure why.

What do cannibals call a body in a hearse?

A movable feast.

Why did the cyclops go to the eye doctor?

He needed a new eyeglass.

Why do banshees scream when someone dies?

The dead are usually hard of hearing.

Why did E.T. go broke?

He phoned home once too often.

What do body snatchers call moving a corpse from the morgue to the graveyard?

Take-out food.

Why don't lepers like being out in the sun?

Their backs peel.

What do you call a goblin who stubs his toe?

A hobblin' goblin.

Why did the goblin family buy a Chevy?

They were tired of driving Gremlins.

What do you get when you mix a cyclops, a unicorn, and the defensive front line of the Minnesota Vikings?

A one-eyed, one-horned, purple people eater.

What's a cyclops's favorite James Bond movie?

For Your Eye Only.

What's a cyclops's favorite news show?

"Eyewitness News."

Why does a cyclops hate baseball?

It hurts to keep its eye on the ball.

What did the leper do when she was surprised by the ghost?

She jumped out of her skin.

Three things you should never tell a leper:

1. Shake a leg.

2. Lend me a hand.

3. Lend me your ear.

What do lepers do when they're out of money in poker games?

They play their hands.

Why is it tough for fire-breathing dragons to eat out?

They have to find a place that has a smoking section.

What's the toughest thing about being a fire-breathing dragon?

> *Being able to afford all the throat lozenges.*

What's a dragon's favorite love song?

> *"Stop Dragon My Heart Around."*

Why did the pet snake hate its owner?

> *He was a real person in the grass.*

What's a snake's favorite song?

> *"Fangs for the Memories."*

Why does the mortuary beautician never rush to work?

> *Her clients aren't in any hurry.*

What do you get when you cross a gargoyle with a zombie?

A dim-witted gargoyle.

LEPERDY!

ANSWER:

MR. POTATO HEAD, A YUGO, AND A HIDEOUS UNDERGROUND MONSTER.

QUESTION:

WHAT'S A SPUD, A DUD, AND A C.H.U.D.?

What's a cannibal's favorite sitcom?

> *"Ate Is Enough."*

What's the difference between a gargoyle and
a tourist?

> *One's a frightening creature with big
> teeth and a potbelly, and the other's a
> decoration on a building.*

What do you call the spirit of a dead chicken that haunts a house?

A poultry-geist.